easy piano
play-along
► Chart Hits

Wise Publications
part of The Music Sales Group
London / New York / Paris / Sydney / Copenhagen / Berlin / Madrid /Hong Kong/ Tokyo

Published by
Wise Publications
14-15 Berners Street,
London W1T 3LJ, UK.

Exclusive Distributors:
Music Sales Limited
Distribution Centre, Newmarket Road,
Bury St Edmunds, Suffolk IP33 3YB, UK.
Music Sales Pty Limited
20 Resolution Drive, Caringbah,
NSW 2229, Australia.

Order No. AM1001660
ISBN 978-1-84938-693-7

Music processed by Camden Music.
Arranged by Christopher Hussey.
Edited by Oliver Miller.
Cover design by Ruth Keating.

Printed in the EU.

Your Guarantee of Quality
As publishers, we strive to produce every book to the
highest commercial standards.
This book has been carefully designed to minimise awkward
page turns and to make playing from it a real pleasure.
Particular care has been given to specifying acid-free, neutral-sized paper
made from pulps which have not been elemental chlorine bleached.
This pulp is from farmed sustainable forests and was
produced with special regard for the environment.
Throughout, the printing and binding have been planned to
ensure a sturdy, attractive publication which should give years of enjoyment.
If your copy fails to meet our high standards,
please inform us and we will gladly replace it.

www.musicsales.com

BAD ROMANCE (LADY GAGA)

Words & Music by Stefani Germanotta & RedOne

With confidence ♩ = 119

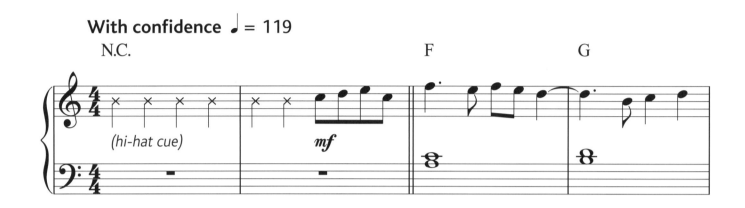

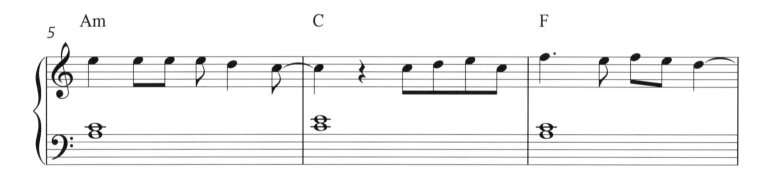

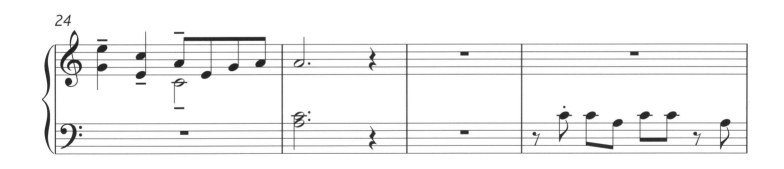

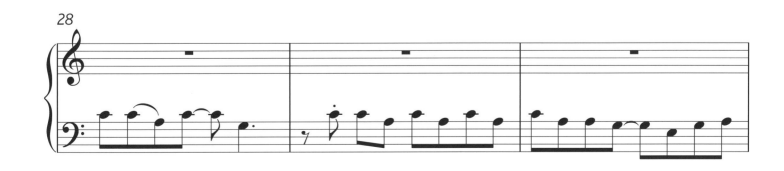

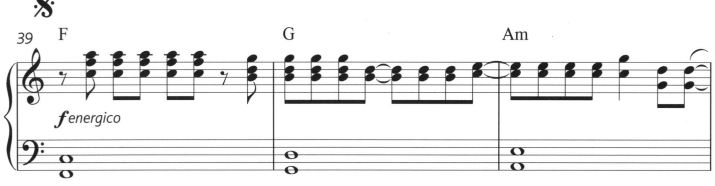

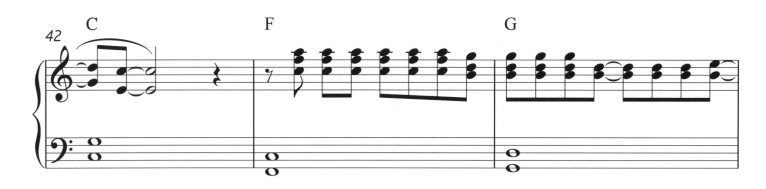

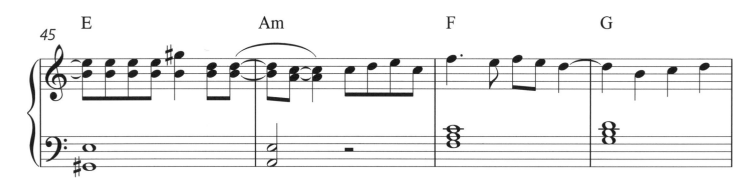

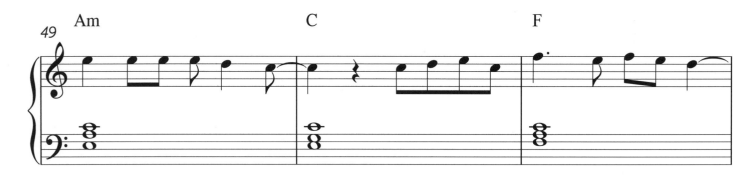

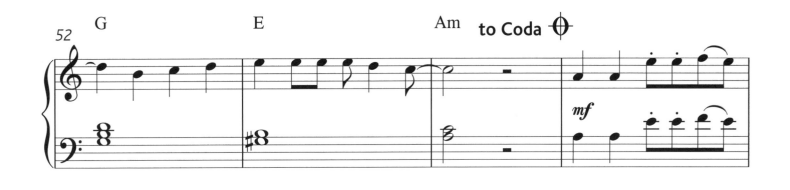

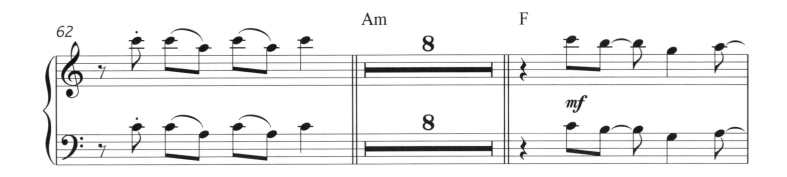

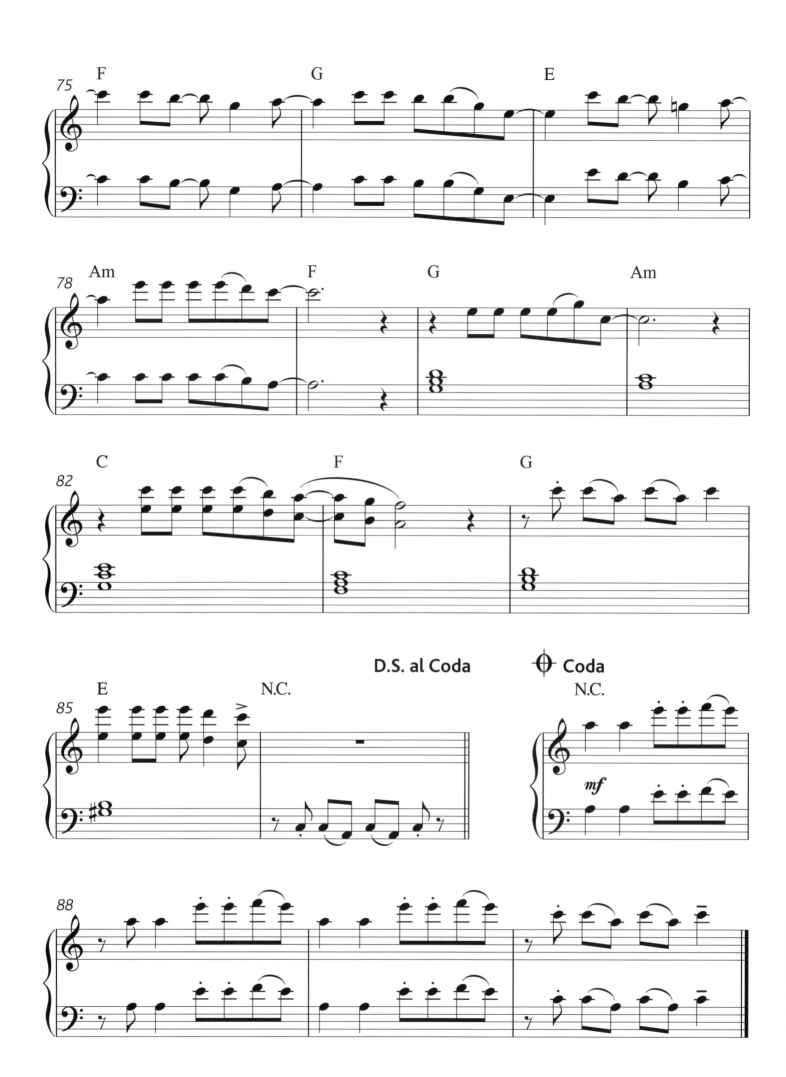

D.S. al Coda

Coda

BROKEN STRINGS (JAMES MORRISON)

Words & Music by James Morrison, Fraser T. Smith & Nina Woodford

CHASING PAVEMENTS (ADELE)

Words & Music by Adele & Eg White

Tenderly ♩ = 80

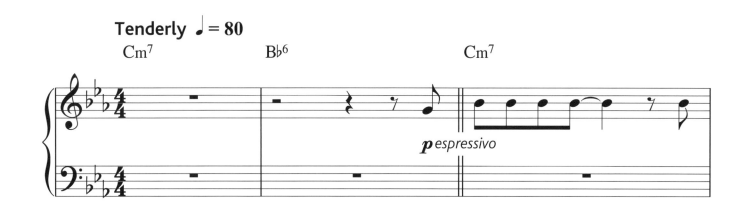

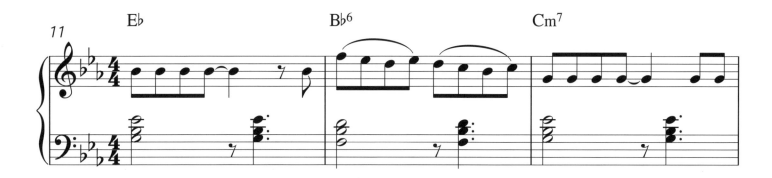

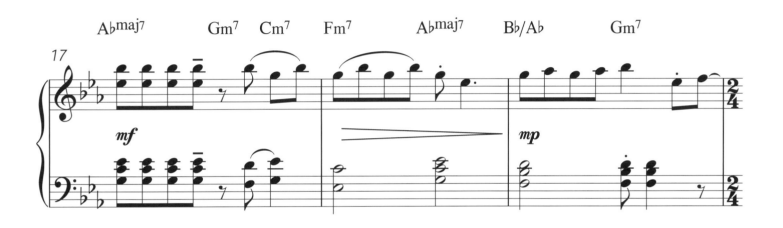
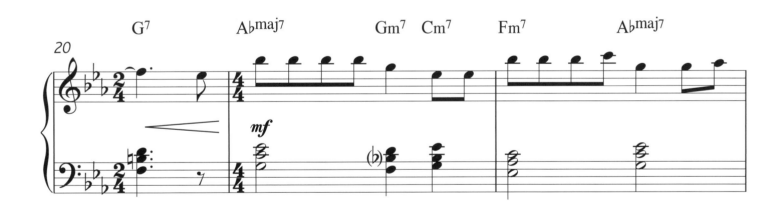
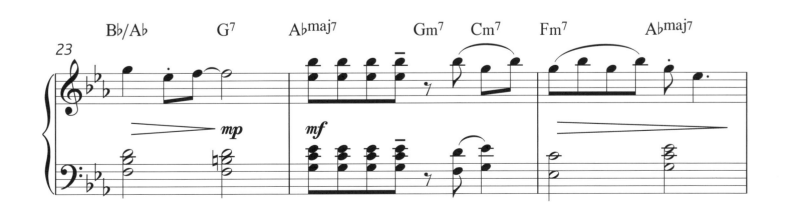

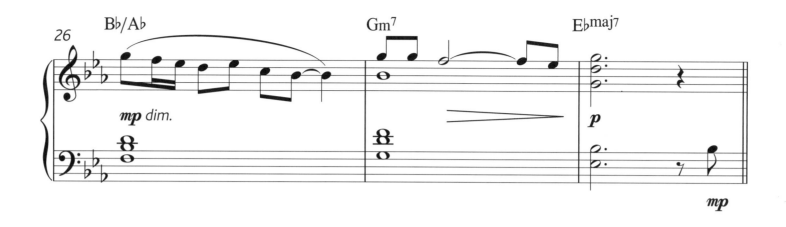

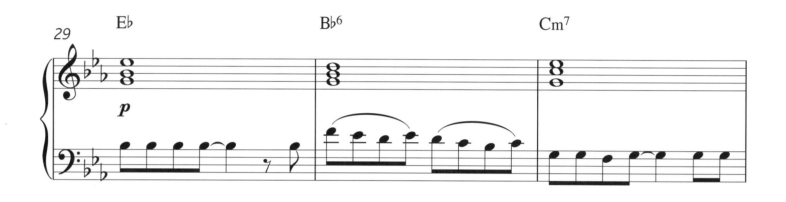

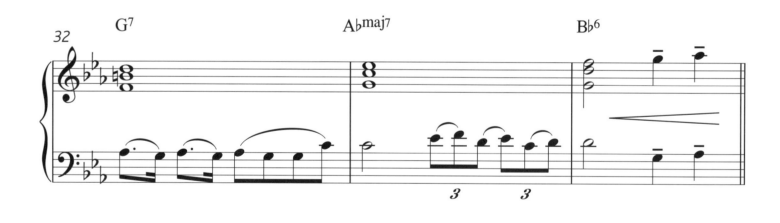

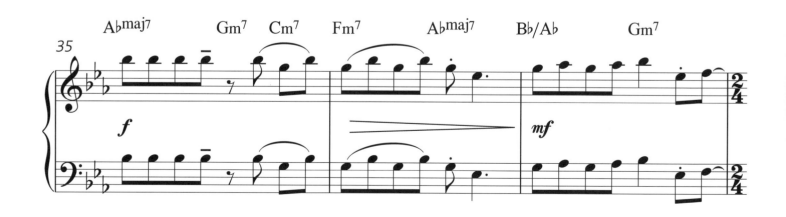

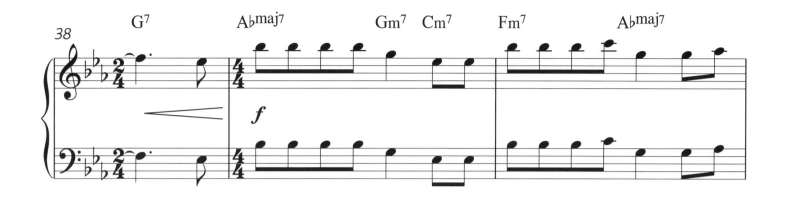

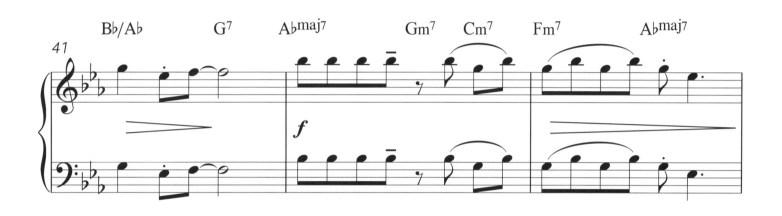

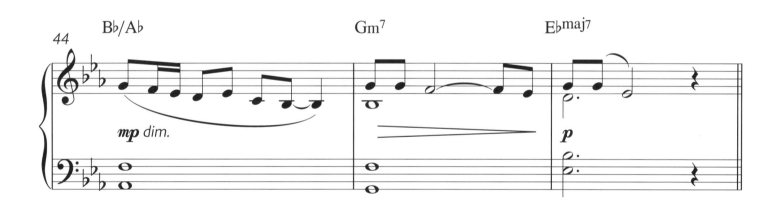

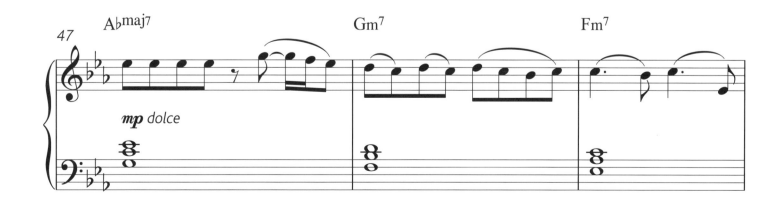

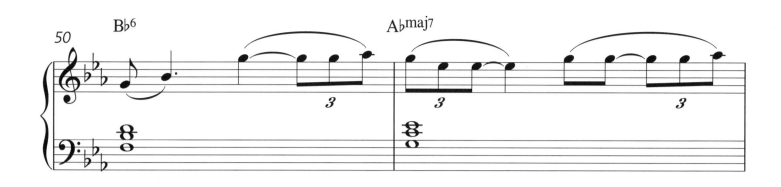

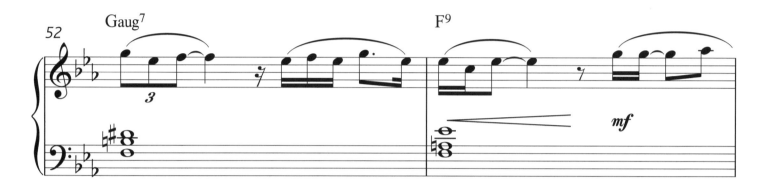

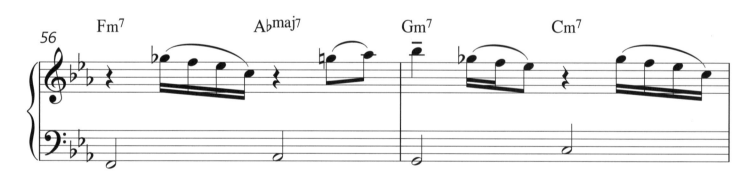

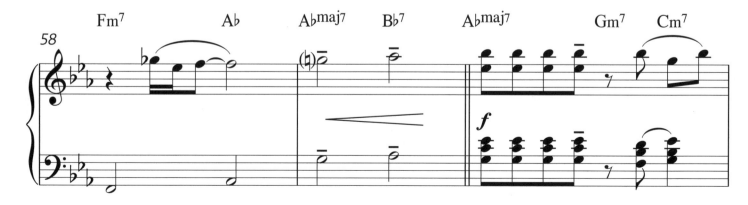

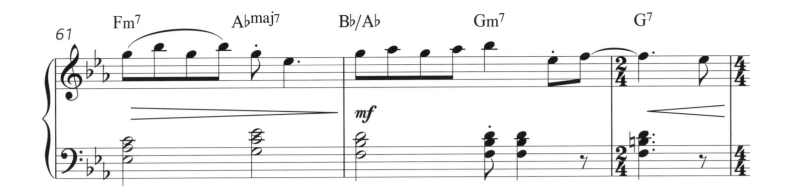

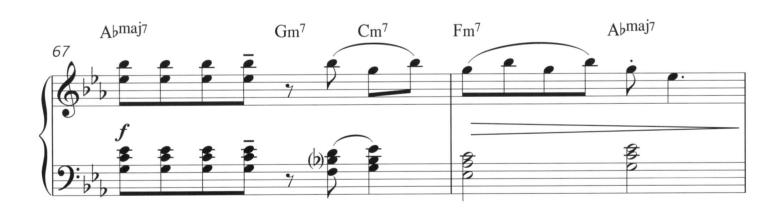

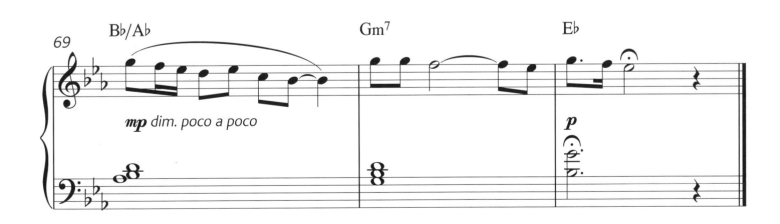

THE CLIMB (JOE MCELDERRY)

Words & Music by Jessica Alexander & Jon Mabe

With passion ♩ = 76

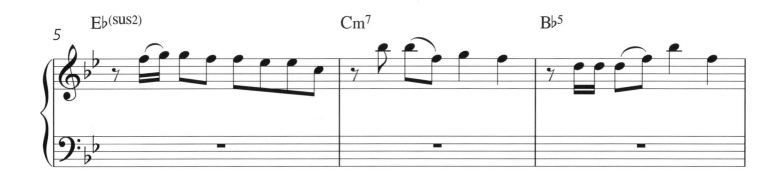

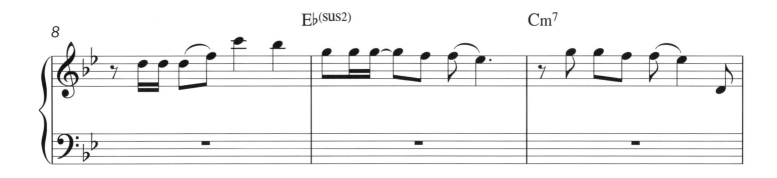

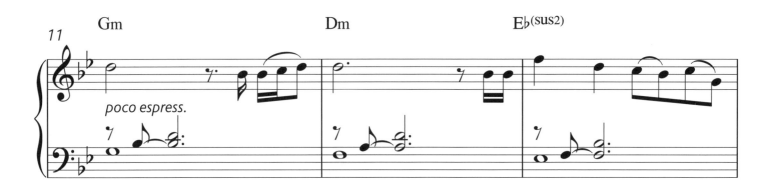

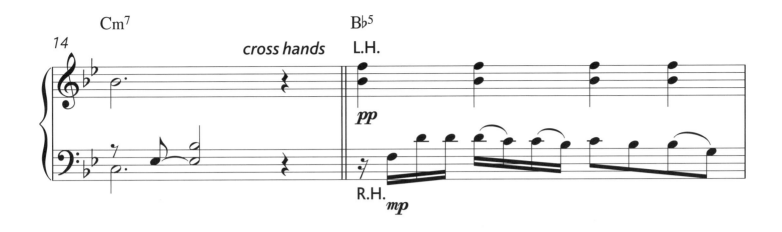

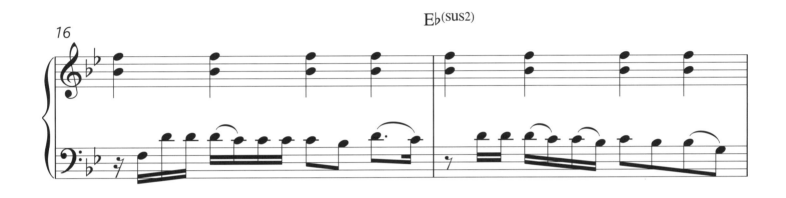

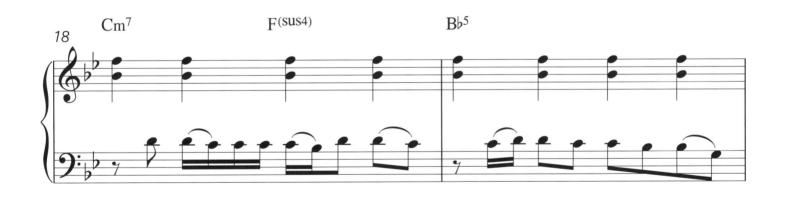

Slightly faster (♩ = 79)

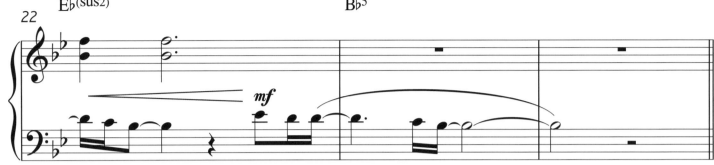

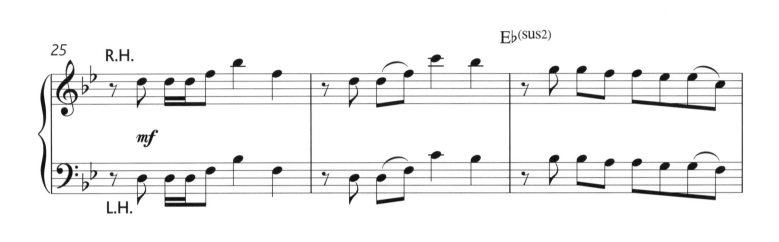

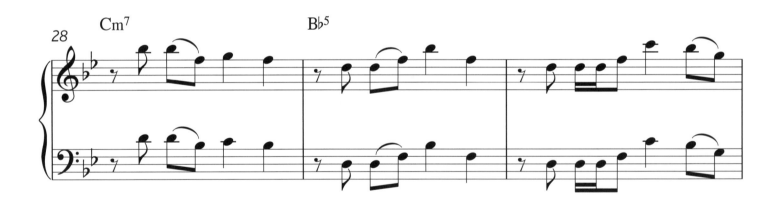

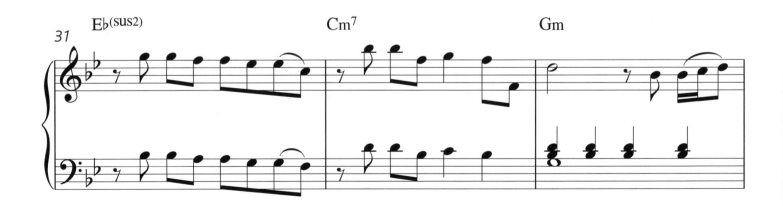

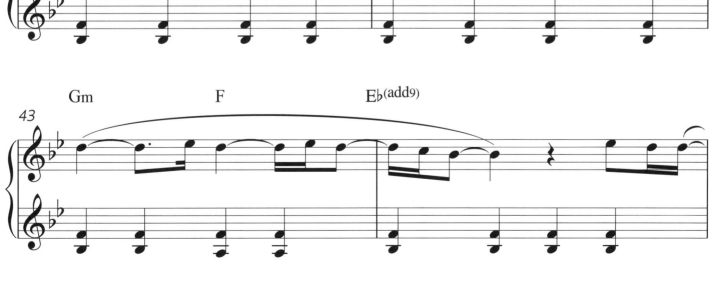

CRY ME OUT (PIXIE LOTT)

Words & Music by Pixie Lott, Mads Hauge, Phil Thornalley & Colin Campsie

Smoothly, with tenderness ♩. = 60

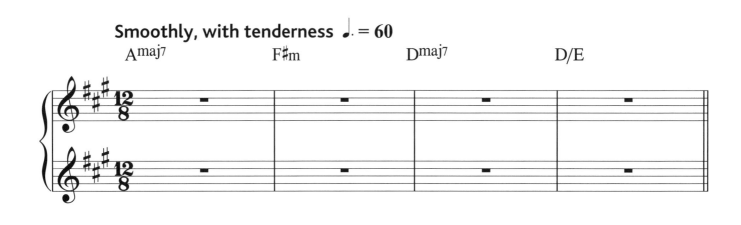

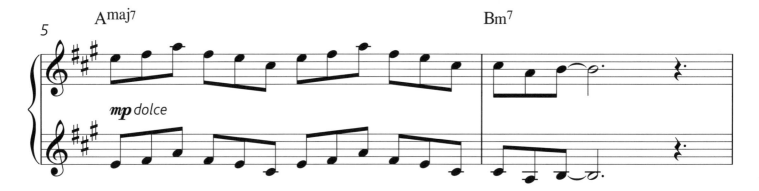

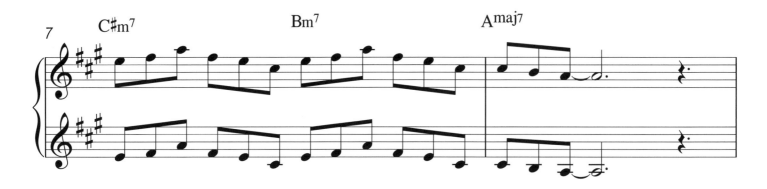

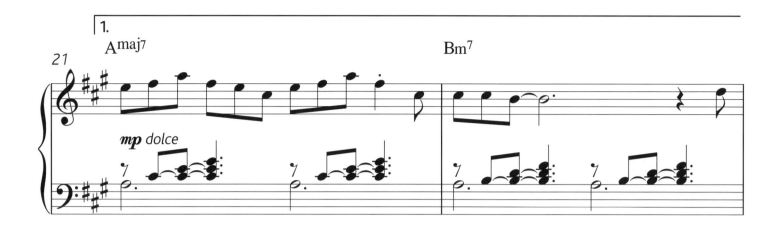

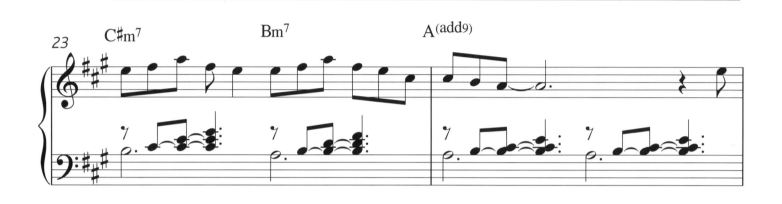

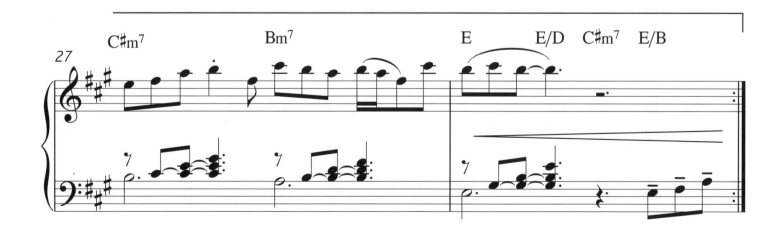

Hallelujah (Alexandra Burke)

Words & Music by Leonard Cohen

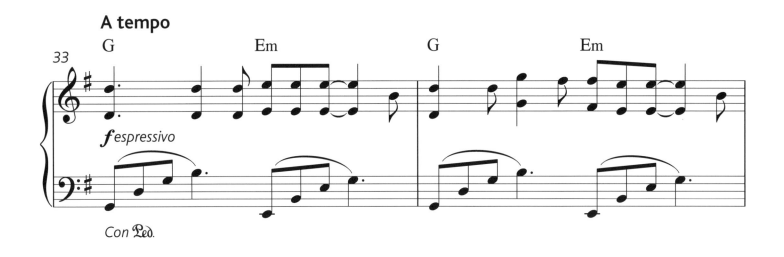

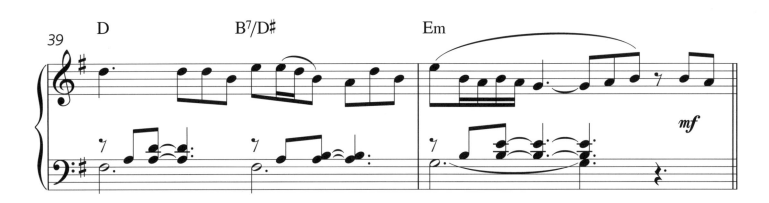

LOVE STORY (TAYLOR SWIFT)

Words & Music by Taylor Swift

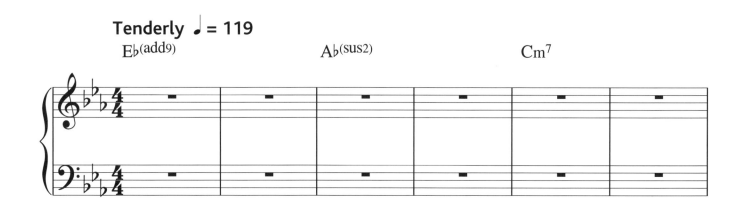

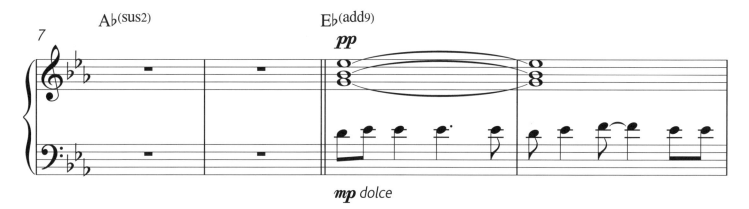

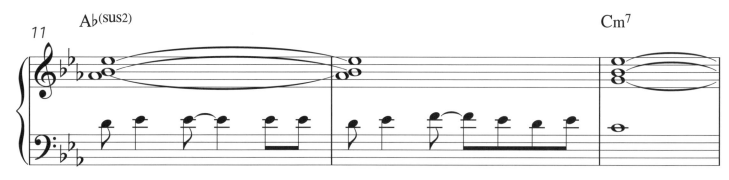

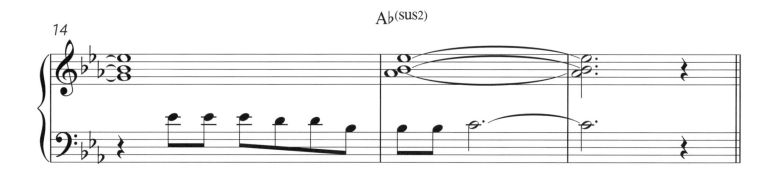

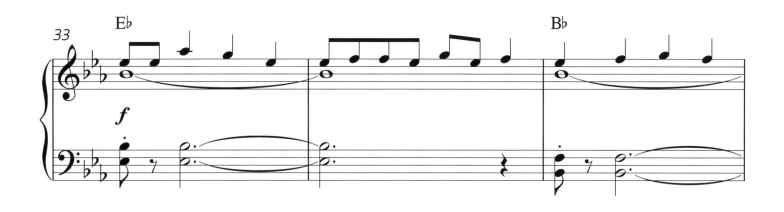

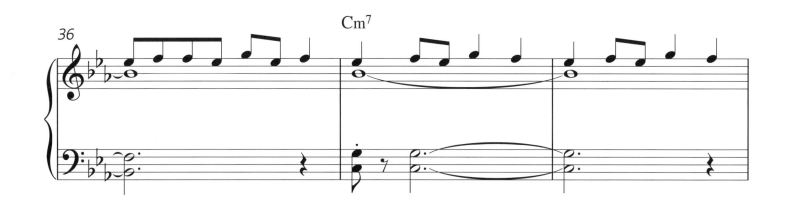

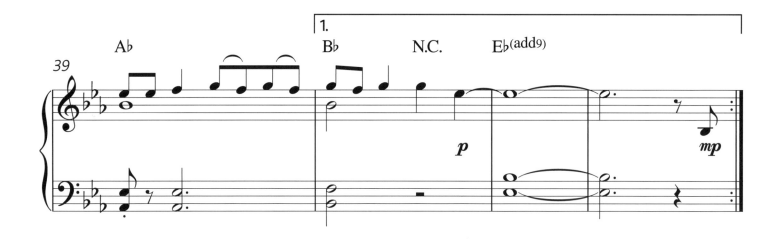

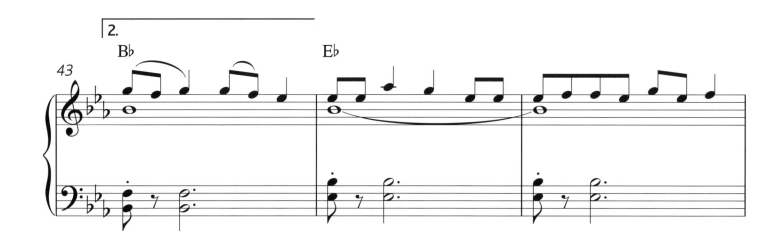

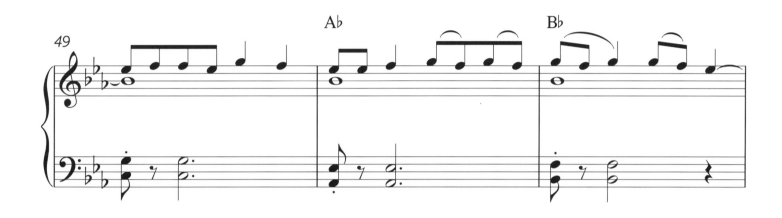

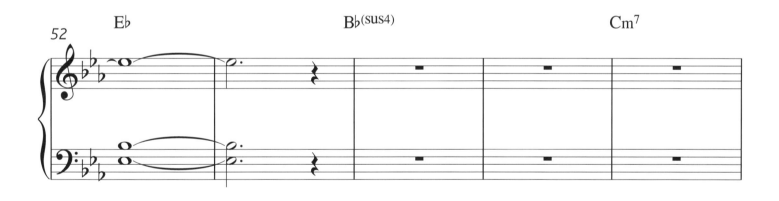

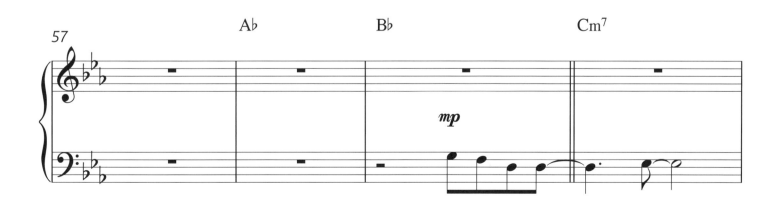

RUN (LEONA LEWIS)

Words & Music by Gary Lightbody, Jonathan Quinn, Mark McClelland, Nathan Connolly & Iain Archer

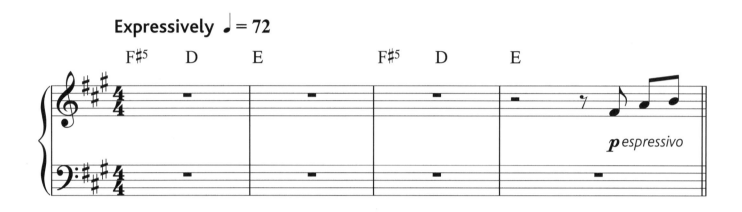

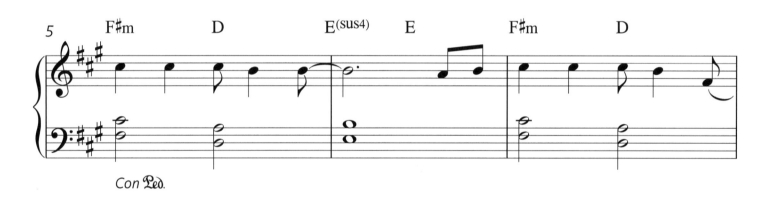

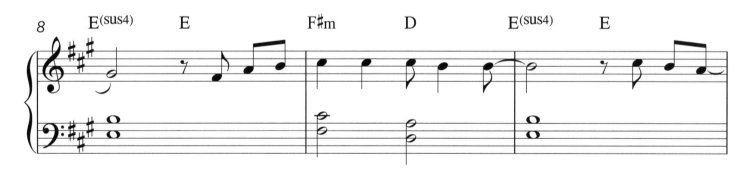

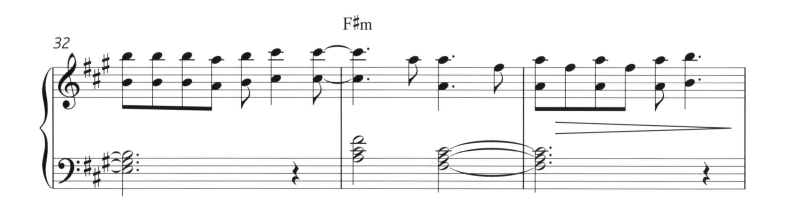

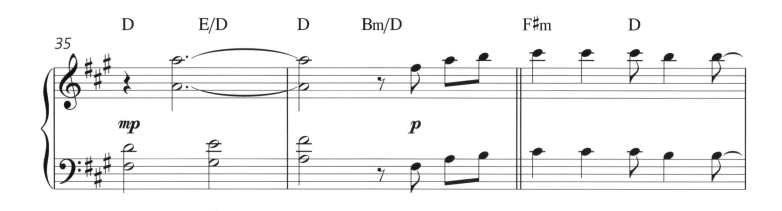

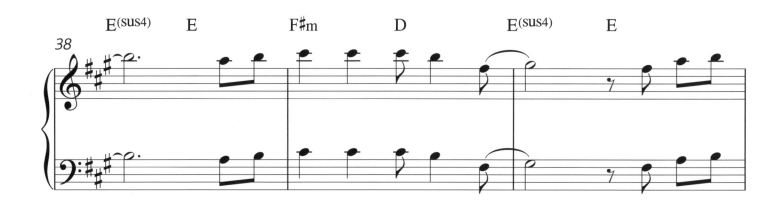

44

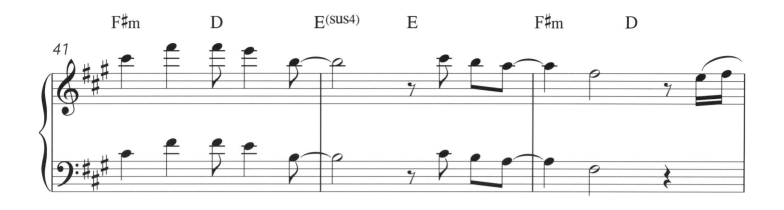

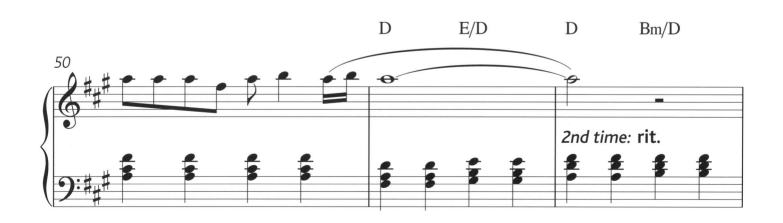

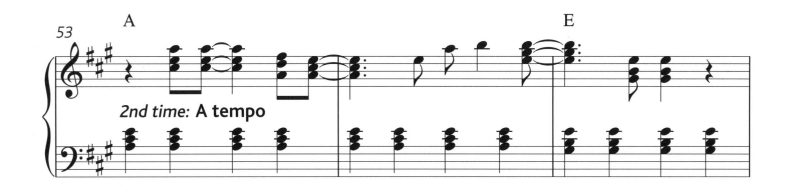

2nd time: **A tempo**

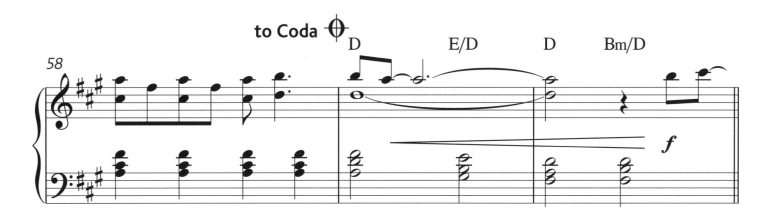

to Coda

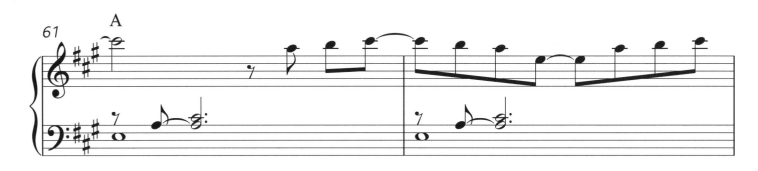

molto rit.

1 2 3 4 5 6 7 8 9

CD Tracklisting

Demonstration Tracks

1 **Bad Romance**
(Germanotta/RedOne)
Sony/ATV Music Publishing (UK) Limited

2 **Broken Strings**
(Morrison/Smith/Woodford)
Chrysalis Music Limited/
Sony/ATV Music Publishing

3 **Chasing Pavements**
(Adele/White)
Universal Music Publishing Limited

4 **The Climb**
(Alexander/Mabe)
Stage Three Music Limited/
Warner/Chappell Artemis Music Limited

5 **Cry Me Out**
(Lott/Hauge/Thornalley/Campsie)
Universal Music Publishing MGB Limited/
Sony/ATV Music Publishing (UK) Limited

6 **Hallelujah**
(Cohen)
Sony/ATV Music Publishing (UK) Limited

7 **Love Story**
(Swift)
Sony/ATV Music Publishing (UK) Limited

8 **Run**
(Lightbody/Quinn/McClelland/Connolly/Archer)
Kobalt Music Publishing Limited/
Universal Music Publishing Limited

Backing Tracks

9 **Bad Romance**

10 **Broken Strings**

11 **Chasing Pavements**

12 **The Climb**

13 **Cry Me Out**

14 **Hallelujah**

15 **Love Story**

16 **Run**

To remove your CD from the plastic sleeve,
lift the small lip to break the perforations.
Replace the disc after use for convenient storage.